BE
OPEN

Narmada Rao

Psychologist, NLP Trainer, Coach

ISBN 979-8-89610-769-9

Dedication

Always, to the man behind everything good in my life! My Dad!

Late Shri K. Madhava Rao

(Dec. 1952 to Dec. 2014)

Preface

For those familiar, this is the 4th book in the series of quotes. The first three are Open Up, Open Up-Close, and Just Open. You may be familiar with the story behind too.

For those who are new, here's some context as to why quotes. Remember Shakespeare? Of course, you do! One of the greatest playwrights of all time. My father and my maternal grandfather used to rattle off a few lines from Macbeth, Julius Caesar and more with ease. I used to be spellbound. Those few lines were so striking that I was interested in reading the entire plays themselves.

I have always been intrigued by the power of words and how to say a lot in a little. Hence, this book is the fourth in the Open Up series.

There's always a parallel thought - "How about I expand on each of them and give additional context?" But yet again, I resist the temptation to say more. Why, you ask? When a lot is said and explained, we follow. When a little is said and a lot is left to our imagination, we think. And that's the whole idea in this series. I wish to provoke a thought and evoke a realisation rather than sell my thought and get a buy-in. So, here are some small bites with lots to chew and stew!

I wish you a pleasant read and some healthy reflections.

Best wishes,
Narmada

Acknowledgements

I am always grateful for my pillar of strength, my mother – for being supportive and encouraging.

It's never a one-person journey. Hence, I am also indebted to all those who have impacted me and propelled me to think, feel and therefore write!

Most importantly, I am eternally grateful to the almighty for the divine grace, blessings, and guidance.

A hero is the central character of a story.
Which means, in your life,
you can't help but be the hero,
whether you want it or not,
whether you accept it or not!
What kind of a hero you want to be
is left up to you.
- Victim hero – the one who feels they are
mainly at the receiving end of life!
- Survivor hero – the one who rises to
survive whatever happens in life!
- Action hero – the one who feels most
people deserve a punch to be set right!
- Comic hero – the one who feels
everything has to be made funny and light!
(contd...)

\- Helping hero – the one who feels they
are next in line to God to help!
\- Kind hero – the one who feels kindness
is the gift they'd like to give to all they
meet!
\- Gracious hero – the one who recognizes
everyone
and makes them believe they are
heroes, too!
\- Passive hero – the one who wants life to be
better without doing much about it!
Which one are you currently?
Which one would you like to be?

When you wait for good things to happen,
you live in hope.
When you believe that only good things
will happen, you are optimistic.
When you do the best you can every
minute, you are committed.
Those are the ones who live without
regret because they always give their best,
regardless of the outcomes!

Don't fall for people who want to build
temples for you.
Those who keep you on a pedestal have
some standard for you to live up to, failing
which, you fall to the ground.
Those who have levelled the playing
ground will be with you all around.

Who are you trying to prove to, and what
are you trying to prove about?
What happens when you prove?
And how long will its effect last?
What happens if you don't prove too?
Whatever you do, if you do well, your
point is proven anyway.
It takes a lot more energy to prove
something than do something.

The sight of a helpless, old, destitute
might trigger sympathy in one,
compassion in another;
indifference in one and
inspiration in another.
The sight is a mere trigger that rekindles
what is already active and alive within
you.

Once it is over, it is not between you and
them, or you and what happened.
It is between you and you!
The part of you that wants to heal and be
happy versus the part of you that wants to
hold on and feel miserable.

The more fears, the greater the propensity
to judge.
So, when you are afraid of judgments, you
are, in essence, afraid of others' fears.
We can be scared of danger, but it doesn't
make sense to be fearful of fear itself,
does it?

Don't be a mouthpiece for those
who can talk.
You'll make them mute in time!
Don't be a crutch for those who can walk.
You'll make them lame in time!
Don't be a solution provider for those who
can think.
You'll make them mindless in time!
Enable them to find their resources,
and they will be competent in time!

Don't believe yourself!
Instead, believe 'in' yourself.
When you believe yourself,
you believe all your mind's stories.
When you believe in yourself,
you believe in your abilities to learn and
move forward.

A good photograph is not only about the
subject but also the composition!
Likewise, life, too!
Focus on the entire picture!
And not only on the object of interest or
desire.

Before declaring what you can do to help them, check what they are willing to do for themselves.

Conversations with therapists shouldn't be to compensate for the lack of relationships. They should be to aid you in finding meaningful relationships.

Everyone has a story, a weight.
Some choose to show it as a baggage and
feel weighed down by it.
Some see it as an opportunity to lift and
feel stronger with it.

With every stroke of bad luck,
get better, not bitter!

Don't hurt the spirit
and feed the body!

Expecting others to understand your pain
delays your capacity to heal yourself.
People's understanding will only give you
a sense of satisfaction - not healing!

Give those who are willing a chance,
and not only to those who are talented.
Their willingness will make them shine
brighter than the brightest talent.
And in doing so, you are giving rise to
newer talent.

He who tries to make life difficult for others is, in essence, making his own life difficult.

Fame can't be the objective behind what you do.
It can be an outcome of what you do.

Remember, it is just feedback. Don't make a mental disease out of it by dwelling on it in an unresourceful way!

If a person is making you beg,
be certain that their attachment to
their ego is greater than the
love for you.

If fear is high and awareness is low,
your life would go in doubts and regrets.

Just as you wouldn't keep track of the recycling history of the junk from your past, let go of the need to check on the progress of your ex, too. It doesn't serve you.

Keep a safe distance from those who
willfully abandon you in pain.
Someone prioritising their comfort over
your pain isn't worth the bargain.

I am grateful when life is fair.
I am humbled when it isn't.

If judging is the first thing you do,
that's fine!
So long as the second thing that you do is
question that judgment!

An independence that creates
self-reliance is helpful.
But if it creates self-indulgence –
think again.

Is it actually love, or are you simply bound?

The world takes you more seriously
when you are steady, not angry!

If you think of yourself as an insect,
someone will crush you eventually.
If you consider yourself God,
they will expect you to grant their wishes
unconditionally.
If you think of yourself as another soul on
this planet,
you can coexist peacefully.

When you exercise, you become strong.
What you exercise becomes stronger.
What are you exercising frequently -
anger, fear, hurt, gratitude, love or joy?
None have a strength of their own.
It is what you give them.

While speaking of consequences,
maintain a sequence.
First, discuss the issue at hand, seek to
understand, and then expand on the
implications.
Never the other way around.

When we are not ready to face something,
avoidance is at the top of our minds.
Not action.
Hence, when action is required, what we
give is a reaction.

Don't be a fan.
Be a worthy fan.
If they are your inspiration,
you must be inspired to improve.
Simply singing their glories won't make a
difference.

If you don't acknowledge the universe in
all its goodness,
it gets tricky for you to manifest
what you want.

We sometimes wait for signs to become
warnings and alarms before acting on
them.
Not because we don't know the
consequences! But because we want some
attention or to appear heroic.
Ironically, prevention doesn't get the kind
of attention that reversing gets!

While asking for help, be clear on what
you need help with.
Don't wait for the universe to figure it out.
The more precise you are, the faster you
get help.

If you belong to a good place yourself,
no one can make you feel bad.

A little appreciation, acknowledgement, and understanding can go a long way in helping a tired horse run a tough race.

Learn to channel your people-pleasing
skills dynamically so that the one who is
pleasing and the one you intend to please
- both win!

Never make an account statement when
you are bitter,
as you will recall only those things that
make you feel further bitter.

No one is interested in knowing how well
you can scold yourself.
It would be inspiring to see how
committed you are to change yourself.

Only a peaceful person can respond
peacefully.
Anyone who is not at peace must be in
some sort of pain because it is painful not
to be peaceful.

Rather than expecting gratitude from
those who may have forgotten you,
express gratitude to those you remember.
Gratitude works best when it is expressed
rather than expected!

If someone tells you that you are the source of their happiness, it means they haven't figured out how to be happy yet. Don't be pleased with it; rather, be concerned.

Anger is what you feel - not who you are!
Fat is what you have - not who you are!
Procrastination is what you are doing - not
who you are!
Don't identify yourself with anything you
don't wish to be.
Observe them as behaviours that need
changing.
And remember that you are beautiful-
that's who you innately are!
The creator has never created bad
products!

It's not about learning new things.
It's about learning something consistently
for so long that you discover depths of
your understanding in new ways every
day. If your focus is on constantly learning
something new, you may be gathering the
dust that lies on the surface rather than
tapping into the wisdom within.

When there's immense pressure, don't
focus on how to survive.
It will create stress as you are viewing it as
a threat.
Focus on how you can thrive; then, you
will view it as an opportunity.

Knowing your story of how you met with
an accident won't necessarily equip the
doctor to find all your wounds.
Take time to know your wounds, fears,
and triggers so that you can start your
healing journey rather than expect others
to deal with them.

Once a dog is used to sleeping next to you,
it won't return to its kennel even if you
want it to.
There's a place for everyone, including
you!
If you smudge the lines now for whatever
reasons, you'll find it difficult to
reestablish them later.
And they will find it unnecessary to
follow them.

What kind of kind are you?
If you are egotistically kind, you will keep
track of your kindness and feel bad if it
isn't reciprocated.
If you are fearfully kind, you may worry if
the other person deserves your kindness,
and if they may take you for granted.
If you are genuinely kind, you won't be
affected by what others do or say, as it is
your nature.

Being in a relationship is not about gaining
ownership rights for people, their space,
or their time.
It is about relinquishing the thoughts
of ownership and replacing that with
trust.

Consistency comes into the picture only
when you think of the past or the future.
Can you think of the present alone and do
what you have to do?
Consistency will not be your concern if
you take care of 'now'.

Don't measure your success or your
weight daily.
It will keep you from moving ahead.
Only measure your efforts and monitor if
you are moving toward your outcomes.

When life throws a setback, it wants you
to step back - not give up!
Step back, gain perspective, and move
forward, as this will offer you a fresh
perspective and a shift in track.

If you step out of your shoes, you'll get a perspective.
When you step into their shoes, you get their perspective. That's when the magic of understanding happens.

Confidence may come and go! Faith stays! No confidence in the world can manifest things the way faith does.

Be grateful to that person who walked away without looking back—for teaching you that intense pain in the short run is better than constant pain in the long run. Also, be grateful for that person who tried to stay, waiting for someone to look back—for teaching you that love is not afraid of pain and that a bit of love can overcome even a lot of pain.

When learning to swim, there's always a
likelihood of drowning.
The coach knows knows that but isn't
perturbed by it.
He stands back confidently and asks you
to jump in the deep side.
He knows unless he trusts you and pushes
you, you won't learn.

If you try to fine-tune others without
fine-tuning yourself,
you will soon be out of tune with yourself.
Instead, focus on fine-tuning yourself so
that you easily find people more in tune
with you.

Dwelling in past miseries can make us
acquire a taste for misery.
This acquired taste will make you
unconsciously attract
more miseries.
Hence, leave them where they need to be.

Don't worry about what others think.
Their attention will be diverted by
the next notification they get on their
smartphones. So be smart, think of what
you want to do, and proceed.

Not everyone who offers help will eventually help you because, for some, the excitement to offer is greater than their inclination to fulfil.

Awareness doesn't mean being aware of your space, time, and chair alone. It is about being mindful of everyone in that ecosystem.

You may indeed be too disturbed to be focused.
But it is also equally possible that you can be so focused that you can't be disturbed.

People aren't disappointing you. They are awakening you. How long will you be convinced of your expectations and criteria without noticing reality? Thank those who have awakened you to reality.

Our disappointment in others increases
when we are already disappointed with
ourselves.
When you find yourself dependable,
other disappointments won't get you.

Our first limitation in seeing others is our
inability to see beyond ourselves.

Pain becomes suffering when we attach
our judgments to it.

Perspectives don't change with a change
in sight.
They change when we challenge what we
think is right.

Rejection is a process of selection.
Even if it comes across as discrimination,
it is each person's right to
self-determination.

Relationships don't fail because people express themselves.
Relationships fail because people don't know how to express themselves in ways that are healthy and helpful.

Singularly, we may not feel abundant.
Collectively, we cannot experience scarcity.
Together, we are always abundant!

Stop trying to put up with things.
Either make things work,
mend it, make peace with it,
or move out of it.
But don't put up with anything anymore.
You aren't helping anyone, including
yourself.

Talking of illness doesn't get you closer
to good health,
just like focusing on what you don't want
won't get you closer to what you really
want!

When it is important, it can't be further classified as easy or difficult. It is important! That's it!

There are places where you have to make
decisions and places where you have to
take opinions.
Using either one all the time creates
stress.

Treat mixed signals as red flags because the one who is clear will never give you mixed signals.

Unless you are a dependent or a baby,
it's not others' responsibility to take better
care of you.
It is, and always will be, your
responsibility!

Waves hit the hardest where there
are rocks because rocks offer strong
resistance.
When there's no resistance, water flows.

If you don't believe in God because of
science, how come you believe in all your
irrational fears and beliefs
that are not backed by science?

What you say after you are questioned is a
justification.
What you say even before is your
communication.

When it feels like your mind won't listen
to you anymore,
be proactive, and stop listening to it.
Give it something to deal with.
If your mind can play tricks on you,
so can you!

Stay with people when with people,
no matter what your reasons.
Your reasons will exist as long as you do,
but not the people!
So, prioritize well!

One can experience pain without ever understanding the pain of another. It is not pain that makes us compassionate, then.
It is self-pity versus humanity!
One who thinks - "I didn't deserve this"; versus the other who thinks, "No one should ever go through this."

The confidence that comes from being
right vanishes the minute there's a slight
chance of being wrong.
The confidence that comes from openness
lasts long.

We envy others' success when we don't
bother to know the efforts behind it!
Anyone who cares to know the success
will be inspired, not jealous!

"How could they do it?" and "Why me?" are questions to which even if you get the answers, they will never be satisfactory. Instead, focus on what happened and what needs to happen now.

Appreciation is not everyone's cup of tea
because they may be suffering from
inadequacy.
Hence, don't expect an empty cup to fill
your cup.
Fill it up yourself, please!

A good performer may not necessarily
make a good teacher.
A performer likes to be at the forefront,
but a teacher has to be the backbone
facilitating the learner.

Don't mistake
a controlling person for a person in
control;
a quiet person for a calm person;
a person who agrees, for a person who
understands.
When it comes to humans, unlike
machines, there are no standard templates
to follow.
Observe, understand and proceed!

Don't blame others for their inability to help themselves when you are unable to stop yourself from running your rescue operations.

Anyone with a 'no response' is
equal to a 'NO' as their response.

Be sharp, not like a knife that cuts, but an
intelligence that shines.

Refrain from rating your teacher.
Rather, improve your ability to learn from
any teacher.

When people seem to be questioning,
they aren't necessarily questioning you.
They are clarifying based on their past
baggage.

Determine who you want to be
before you step out of your house.
Else, the world will dictate who you
should be.

A simple way to know where to keep
people in your life without much effort:
Keep them where they choose to be.
Whatever their recurrent actions are,
those are their unconscious ways of
communicating where they choose to be
in your life.
So, have them accordingly.

It's time we stopped talking about things
to get attention.
Instead, let's speak of things that need our
attention!

When you feel you are being tested
beyond your limits,
life is helping you realise that you are
beyond those limits.

Truly good are those people who don't think that good things have to happen to them for them to be good.

Trying to dominate domination leads to
more aggression.
Understand the reason behind it, and you
will find a way to work around it.

What you are unwilling to change about
yourself, you convince yourself by saying
life demands you to be that way.

Don't turn to spirituality because you
want to avoid humanity.
Learning to co-exist with compassion is
the first step of spirituality.

When you are down, don't look for
sympathy or empathy.
Look for inspiration!

Being smart can't be a ruse for being
loved.
To be loved, we have to be loving.

Either decide that you want to stay in
misery and enjoy it!
Or decide to snap out of it and do
whatever it takes for it.
But don't fool yourself by saying you will
work on it because others want you to do
something about it.
You won't do it unless you want it!

You don't pray to remind God of your existence.
You pray to remind yourself of God's presence.

It might appear easier to live in denial
than to deal with something.
But it isn't so. Deal with things before
they become deal-breakers.

You don't need self-love.
Love will do!
When there's love in your heart, it will
naturally touch you first. If you can't feel
it toward yourself, then what you show
toward others may be attachment rather
than love.

While walking away, always know what
you are walking towards.
Otherwise, you may find yourself walking
back towards the very thing you walked
away from.

Don't use your suffering as an excuse
to get away or get the right of way.

Excessive compliance is detrimental to growth.

Feel bad to the extent that it reminds you
to be good.
Not to the extent that it makes you doubt
that you are any good.

Don't use adjectives while offering criticisms.
And never fail to use adjectives while giving appreciation.

When one doesn't intend to cross the
bridge, the water is not the problem.
Don't offer bridges to those who don't
wish to cross.
They will break it to prove their point.

However much they love you, they can't
give you what you want.
They can only give you what they have.
In the name of love, we can't expect or
demand what they don't have.

If you keep testing yourself, you will only get evaluations.
When you trust yourself, you get results.

Is your ego protecting you from
getting hurt in the future?
Or preventing you from healing from the
past?

Kindness works if one is steady with it.
Sudden bouts of kindness can
attract more doubt than gratitude.

You can't be good or bad at meditation!
You are either meditating or you are not!
The more you evaluate, the less you
meditate!

When you feel you are going through
something for no fault of yours,
that's a secret sign that you are being
saved from something worse.

No relation in your life exists without
your permission.
You are 50% responsible for every
equation in your life.
Unless you change, nothing will change.

If people change their commitment at the speed at which they change their opinions, then you need to change your direction.

When you set expectations with people,
you must communicate and reset them as
you change.
Don't expect people to auto-adjust.

Some want to learn.
And some want to learn on their terms.
The former learn anyway.
The latter learn the hard way!

Separation won't magically make
a relationship better unless you do
something to resolve the differences.
Otherwise, it simply makes you get used
to living without them.

Repeated apologies for the same reason are not a sign of learning! They are a warning sign for the receiver.

In trying to teach, don't traumatise!
Doing so makes even the worthiest
learning futile and the most willing
student resistant.

Your achievement is not your success,
your persistence is!
Your failure is not your drawback,
you giving up is!

If you keep incentivising everything,
they will soon lose motivation for
anything.
Let meaning and purpose supersede
incentives.

Don't try to prove your miseries to the world. It will make it even more miserable. Show yourself that you have better things to do than focus on misery.

You will stop comparing when you realise
that your uniqueness is worth exploring.

When your emotions are misplaced,
there's no point trying to get your words
right.
Align your emotions, and words will
automatically follow.

Learning can be accidental or incidental. But unless you are intentional, you won't sustain either.

It's not all or always about exchanging
energies.
It's about sustaining them, too.

Don't forsake all relationships for the sake of one. Recognise each for its own.

Distraction is not something you do for
yourself; it is something you do to escape
from yourself.
What you do for yourself is called
engagement.

Before you call anyone dominating, check if you are intimidated by their belief in themselves or if they are indeed dictating terms to you.

As lonely as a boat may be,
it can still help someone cross the ocean
safely.

Curiosity is a great skill to foster.
But our expectations kill it.

A wrong relationship can either take
you back or propel you forward in your
development.
It all depends on how you choose to
process it!

It is the pursuit of humanity that delivers happiness.
The pursuit of individual happiness overrides humanity!

Just because our plans look more familiar doesn't mean they are better than life's plans for us.

If you are hoping, hope that you will find your way rather than hope that others will change their way.

Don't try to prepare yourself for what might happen - life is preparing you anyway.

Are people taking you for granted, or have you granted yourself excessively to them?

If you like the truth, you will be open to
perspectives.
If you like your truth, you might be
offended by other perspectives.

It's not about what is convincing.
What's convenient is what's convincing
for most.

Let your good intentions dictate your
actions, not others!

The more desperate you are, the more doubtful they will be to consider your request.

Rebellion is good so long as it is
preceded by reasoning.

Rather than focusing on making good
impressions, focus on good impact.
While impressions may fade, impact stays.

Silence isn't strength,
neither does it denote peace -
when it is used to avoid situations.

Situations and others are as strong as your
fears. Else, you are strong.

The one who searches is limited by his
search criteria.
The one who observes grasps a lot more.

Skills, talents and actions
should contribute to humanity as our
vision - not our vanity.

When death isn't a choice,
we can't personalize and call it
abandonment.
It is a process of life.

You can always say 'No' and make it work
if you keep your frequency and intensity
low, and your empathy and intention right.

You can get the best of lessons on how
relationships work.
But the critical question is, do you want to
make your relationship work?

You can't experience abundance if your reference point is always from a past that had scarcity.

It is better to seek help and swim
than stay quiet and drown.

How you pursue your life determines how
tired you get.

If it's an effort to love "now," there's no point taking pride in loving "then".

Never question with an idea to put down anyone. Question in a way that helps them think better.

Do things because you value something and because you feel they will add value. Otherwise, in a world of endless opportunities, we misuse and abuse all of them rather than make good use of any of them.

Connect with people without getting
carried away!

Looking at life with gratitude, it seems like
a series of miracles.
Looking at it with regret makes it appear
like a series of mishaps.

Showing off your strength when the other person is vulnerable is deemed arrogant.

The best things happen when you are
busy doing good things.

Those who think they will be confident
once they get things may get things and
yet not be confident.
Those who are confident, get things.

Evading a question important to someone
doesn't make them forget it.
It makes them remember even more
that you don't consider their criteria
important.

When you think you can't live without someone, and they make it impossible to live with them, they are doing you a favour!
Accept it!

A consequence that makes a difference
will create an understanding.
A consequence that instils fear creates
momentary compliance or brash rebellion.

Healing isn't a separate process.
Healing happens automatically
when you start dealing with life.

Those who like control will look for
predictability. Those who are open will
look for signs.

When we gain independence from our perceptions of likes and dislikes, we become committed to doing what is required.

Even the best of habits aren't as healthy as awareness.

You can choose to sit back and watch.
Or adapt and play.
But you don't have the power to change
the rules in any way.

The day our love for heaven exceeds the
fear of hell, humanity will be heaven.

When you try to be on everybody's good books, you will pretty quickly be off your own books.

You may have nothing to do with a
person's current action.
But their next one is based on your
current reaction.

Your goodness has never landed you in
trouble.
Your naivety may have!
The sooner you understand that,
the faster you get out of it.

No one would find it easy to be with someone who projects that they don't need anyone.

A person who is focused on offering you
only comfort offers neither perspective
nor growth!
Comfort without growth is called
stagnation!

If you read a lot about dogs, you will observe and connect with dogs wherever you go. Likewise, if you read about depression or narcissism, you will only connect with those, not happiness.

Your attachment to your shoe won't make
it stop biting you.

A relationship that begins with a lot of hope and expectations may not last unless it was pursued through the lens of reality.

Consciousness is not for those who are on auto-pilot mode.

Sometimes, our small falls may be life's big favours.

You can't be mad at a mad elephant.
It would help to be sane to be safe around it.

You tried being happy by learning,
travelling, achieving, shopping,
marrying, singing, dancing, parenting etc.
Are you there yet?

Are you giving instructions for your satisfaction or their clarification?

The past is never more important than
you in the present.

Don't spend a lot of effort trying to avoid
pain because it will make you more
susceptible to it.
You don't need to want pain but be willing
to deal with it should it come your way.

If our reasons are reasons,
why do others' reasons appear as excuses?
If our preferences are preferences,
how come others' preferences are
considered obsessions?
When our thoughts and feelings are justified,
why should others' be rationalized?
Acknowledge and move further rather
than disregard and lose rapport!

The sun will shine on you!
But you can't be hiding behind the
curtains then!

There's a difference between being tough
and being difficult.
Life teaches us to be tough, so we get
through tough times.
Being difficult is when we make it
challenging for others to be with us.

You can be hurt by people who you
dearly love.
But never by those who truly love you.

Nothing will appeal to everyone.
That's why even God has disbelievers.

One was blessed with a great sense of humour because they had to endure many tough times.
One was blessed with patience because they had people around them who were impatient.
One was blessed with individuality because they didn't have much support to lean back on.
One was blessed with willpower because they needed it to overcome all their challenges.
One was blessed with kindness as they didn't have many around them who were that kind.

(contd.)

One was blessed with positivity to help them deal with many negativities.
One was blessed with the ability to be submissive to help them deal with a lot of authority.
One was blessed with an independent nature to help them follow their calling.
One was blessed with leadership to help them lead the society.
One was blessed with creativity to help them look at life differently.
We are all blessed, for sure! It is up to us to recognize and use our blessings the way they were meant to be.

Hope you enjoyed the read.
To know more about the author and her
work, please visit: www.masteryourself.in
or,
www.narmadarao.com